# BORDER COLLIE

A CELEBRATION OF MAN'S BEST FRIEND

NEVILLE TURNER

# BORDER

A CELEBRATION
OF MAN'S BEST FRIEND

# COLLIE

**Dalesman**

# FOREWORD

Meg was a Border Collie and very much a part of our family when the children were growing up. Like all Border Collies she was intelligent, faithful and gentle-natured, and brought such joy to our home. I recall one occasion when Christine, my wife, had cooked a rice pudding in a metal dish and served it to the children before I arrived back from work. When they all had had their fill, the dish was surreptitiously put on the floor by one of my sons for Meg to lick clean. I arrived in the empty kitchen and found the dish near the sink and scraped the sides. I discovered later from my amused children that Meg had been there before me. They still relate this on family occasions.

Neville Turner's book is a warm, humorous and thoughtful study of this wonderful breed of dog, full of fascinating information and stunning photographs. Copies have gone to all my four children to remind them of Meg, our wonderful Border Collie, who we sadly lost some years ago.

**GERVASE PHINN**

# INTRODUCTION

I must have driven into a dozen farm-yards every day in the course of my work as a vet in rural practice. And most times, even before I'd found the whereabouts of the farmer, a sheepdog would greet me. Most were friendly. Experience taught me to recognise the ones that weren't. I always had a camera handy, and enjoyed taking a few photos of Border Collies. Over the years the collie picture collection became huge. Here is a selection of my favourite pictures, which, I hope, capture the Border Collie's distinctive appearance, athleticism and heartwarming appeal.

**NEVILLE TURNER**

# PUPPY LOVE

I recently had the delightful experience of spending a morning in a stable with ten eight-week-old collie pups. They had boundless energy in a non-stop playtime. For their amusement they had been provided with a green plastic box, a tup's horn and a child's sledge, all of which proved popular.

The green box was in constant use.

Play-fighting and sibling rivalry was a popular pastime . . .

. . . but there are lots of cuddles too.

The tup's horn made a perfect teething ring.

Here a four month old pup has a successful first outing. The herding instinct is strong. He shows great promise, but ten feet of cord attached to his collar can be used to retrieve the pupil if youthful exuberance gets the better of him.

A six-month old youngster goes for a gallop to burn off some excess energy.

# ON THE LOOKOUT

Dogs that don't have a kennel usually make their home in a cowshed. It's useful to find a hole . . .

. . . to have a look around.

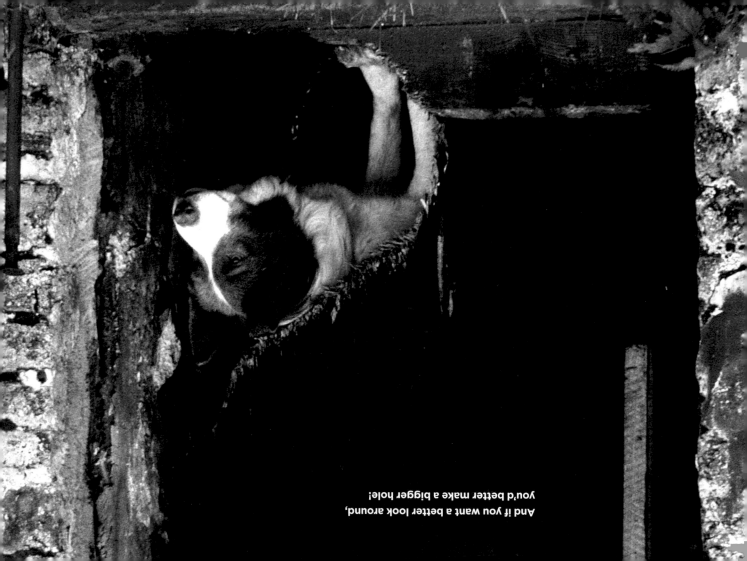

And if you want a better look around,
you'd better make a bigger hole!

This guy was quick as lightning, and accounted for redesigning many a postman's trousers. I never got out of the car on this farm until he'd been shut in.

He lived in a disused water tank.

This fellow could drive a hole straight through the middle of the door.

is to take a strip off the bottom or the door . . .

Another way of tackling the observation problem

. . . and if you're the sociable type, you can make it
big enough for your chum too.

Double doors make the job easier!

It's handy if you have a window . . .

... although there may be noisy
neighbours downstairs!

And then, after two hours of constant activity,
their energy ran out. Within minutes every one
of them fell fast asleep.

. . . even better if you have an
upstairs window . . .

# HOME SWEET HOME

Accommodation-wise, the collies' needs are simple. A waterproof, draughtproof shelter with some clean, dry bedding will suffice. The working dog is seldom kept as a house pet. In fact they seem happier outside in a cobbled together kennel, or in a cosy corner of the cowshed. From there they can keep an eye on everything that's going on in the farmyard.

The ingenuity of the farmer with regard to collie accommodation never ceases to amaze me. Design and construction varies from downright primitive to the height of sophistication. And where there is no purpose-built dwelling, improvisation is the order of the day.

The traditional kennel.

This is a more mode
residence in brushe
aluminium.

Here's a real upmarket kennel which would surely please the council planning department.

I thought Fido was a strange
name for a working dog.
When I asked the farmer why
he'd called his dog Fido, he
replied that his name wasn't
Fido. The name was already
painted on when he bought
the tank at a farm sale.

Here's a friendly welcome.

This dog was a sweetie.
The notice was posted
in the era of his predecessor.
Life isn't fair!

Spot has his name emblazoned by the entrance. He's obviously into 'Home Improvements!' He's also, like many of his kind, into collecting scrap metal.

Diogenes, the Greek philosopher lived in a barrel, although it probably wasn't quite so splendid as this dog's home.

This barrel, however, is a downmarket
version of the Diogenes style — but it
does give him an elevated viewpoint.

There are wooden barrels and metal ones, but they are also available in plastic.

And a plastic barrel that's
big enough for two.

Waterproof, draughtproof, and well bedded. But what an intriguing design.

# ONE MAN AND HIS DOG

At the starting post. The dog is so eager to set off, but he won't move a muscle till the boss says so.

# THE GATHERING

Dogs and men set off at first light to gather the sheep form a vast area of fell. Several hours later they approach the farmstead, the sheep cascading down the hillside like a woolly waterfall.

Five dogs working together without a whistle or word of command. They all know their jobs.

it's naughty to nip . . .

. . . and dangerous too.

Herding skills are mostly used in fields and fells but they are equally useful in the farmyard. Here the flock is being moved though the pens to sort out the sheep before tupping time.

Perfectly choreographed!

Penning is complete, but the dogs keep an eye on the situation.

# COOLING OFF

Gathering can be hot work and the dogs are quick to find a stream or a trough to cool off and have a drink.

The collie's herding ability is not confined to moving sheep. Here we see his skill with poultry.

# HITCHING A LIFT

In a busy working day the collie is only
too ready to hitch a lift on any available
form of transport.

He was a gash an' faithfu' tyke,

As ever lap a sheugh or dyke.

His honest, sonsie, baws'nt face

Aye gat him friends in ilka place;

His breast was white, his touzie back

Weel clad wi' coat o' glossy black;

His gawsie tail, wi' upward curl,

Hung owre his hurdie's wi' a swirl.

from *The Twa Dogs* by Robert Burns